Moonswept Press, Inc.
ISBN: 978-1-60087-001-9

ACKNOWLEDGEMENTS

To My Family, with love.

To Ben, for opening the door to coaching

To Lynn, Lynne,

Terri, Jim, and Sharon,

for showing me an easier, better way.

To all my wonderful clients,

for sharing your journey with me

Thank you!

TABLE OF CONTENTS

HOW DOING YOUR DISSERTATION IS LIKE EATING AN ICE CREAM CONE

Think back a moment to the last ice cream cone you had. Maybe it was a double dip chocolate chip with sprinkles (my favorite!) or simple vanilla. In any case, I would like you to take a moment and think about how you approached eating that ice cream cone.

Did you take a big, deep bite out of it?

How was it to try to swallow that solid lump of cold ice cream? The last time I tried this, I got "brain freeze," a headache, and my teeth hurt. It was not enjoyable.

Compare this with a time when you ate the ice cream in a leisurely manner, taking small bites and licks, slowly and patiently wearing it down. You were, perhaps, lost in the moment, yet focused on the outcome.

How is this related to the dissertation? Many times, graduate students approach the dissertation from the first perspective — they try to bite off huge pieces and cram their way through it, ending up with "brain freeze," headaches, stress, and an unpleasant feeling about the whole thing.

Students who approach the dissertation from the second perspective take longer to wear down the ice cream. They have to be patient, keep track of the melting and drip- ping, but most of all, they have to have faith that they will, indeed, get to the bottom of the scoop.

Break down the dissertation, one small bite at a time, and you too will get to the bottom of the scoop!

HOW TO USE THIS BOOK

This book is designed to be actively used. You may want to read it straight through from beginning to end just to get a feel for all the information and how it's presented. After this, you may want to use the book for "spot relief"- any time you are feeling challenged by one of the issues in this book. For example, if you're feeling in need of some suggestions for boosting creativity, turn directly to this section and try some of the tips until you find one that works.

All of the tips and suggestions in this book are the same ones my clients have used to finish their degrees quickly and easily. Though you and I may have never met, I'd like you to think of me as your dissertation coach- providing you the strategy, support, and structure to help you complete your degree.

I am committed to your success and wish you excellence and ease in your dissertation journey.

SECTION I: PLANNING/GOAL SETTING

When you begin the dissertation process, make certain you do the following:

Pick a topic that you can complete within a year or so.

Many of my clients get caught up in the feeling that the dissertation is *the* seminal work of their lives. And they haven't even graduated yet! There is plenty of time to write *the* definitive work. Just please make sure it's *after* you have the letters Ph.D. after your name.

Pick a committee you feel you can work well with.

Obtain contact information for your advisor and the members of your committee, their preferred methods of contact, and some information on their plans for the next year.

Too often, students select "scary" or "distant" advisors, which, unfortunately, only sets you up for unnecessary anxiety and stress in dealing with them. Choose an advisor who is available, and with whom you can work well. Choose someone who is responsive to what you need and interested in helping you. The same goes for the other members of your committee.

Find out the best days and times to reach them, as well as whether they prefer email, voicemail, or regular mail. Find out approximately how much time they will need in order to give you feedback and provide comments on your work. Also ask if they have any vacations or sabbaticals planned, so you can organize your dissertation year appropriately. Don't wait until the last minute to find out that your advisor may be on sabbatical at the time of your defense. Be proactive and stay "up" on this.

Obtain a copy of your departmental guidelines for completing the dissertation. Read through it and obtain any necessary or supplemental information for your particular project.

These guidelines should provide you with basic information about the usual length, structure, and format of dissertations in your department, as well as important dates and deadlines for graduation.

Bonus Tip:

If it is necessary for your project, obtain the Human Subjects Application as soon as possible. Work on this parallel to writing your proposal. Aim to have the Human Subjects Application almost completed by the time you turn in your proposal. The Internal Review is often the major cause of delay in the proposal process, especially if your topic is sensitive or deals with children or other vulnerable groups.

Obtain copies of several dissertations dealing with your topic. Also obtain one or two dissertations from your department, so that you can use these as more specific models.

Reading or skimming through these will help you formulate your approach and gain a broader understanding of the "feel" or "essence" of a Ph.D.-quality topic and approach. As a bonus, you may also acquire citations, quotes, extra resources, or reference information.

Create a timeline to the completion of your dissertation. Decide when you'd like to finish – and stick to this plan!

Most dissertation projects can be completed within one year, barring any extensive field- work or other specialized circumstances. Use this as a guideline for planning your progress.

Bonus Tip:

A model of how to create a time- line by working backwards can be found in the Appendix of this book. Use this as a model for your own work process.

Make certain you somehow chart or track important dates.

You might want to consider purchasing (or creating) a good size wall calendar to track your progress. This will also allow you to track your progress visually, as mentioned in Section II: Motivation. You don't want to finish up and then find out that you've missed the deadline for graduation.

Utilize the concept of "clustering" or "grouping" similar tasks in planning your work.

It's a good idea to try to perform similar types of work at the same time. For example, try to complete all the research as one task, the organization as another task, and the writing as another task. Shifting back and forth between tasks can result in a loss of efficiency, and an inability to see the "big picture." Grouping similar tasks also cuts down on having to shift between various cognitive modes, which can be mentally taxing.

Allot time to go to conferences, meetings, and seminars during your dissertation year.

Planning time to meet with colleagues and share ideas is a great way to keep your creativity and interest at peak levels. Attending conferences or presenting papers is a rejuvenating change from the research and writing of the dissertation process. As a bonus, it will also strengthen your curriculum vitae and make you more attractive to potential employers.

Plan to schedule a vacation or some time off while your proposal is being reviewed.

Many students have mentioned that writing the proposal is one of the most difficult aspects of the dissertation process. It is a good idea, therefore, to arrange to take a vacation for a few days (or more) while your proposal is being reviewed. This time away will allow you to relax and regroup for the next phase of work.

Set SMART goals.

Goals should be Specific, Measurable, Attainable, Realistic, and Time specific. The more SMART goals you set, the more successful you will be. One example of a SMART goal: "I will write five pages of Chapter One in this next two-hour block." This goal is Specific (What will you do? Write.), Measurable (How much will you do? Five pages.), Attainable (Is this possible? Yes.), Realistic (Is this reasonable for the time frame? Yes.), and Time Specific (By when will you accomplish this goal? The next two hours.).

Bonus Exercise: Set three to five SMART goals to accomplish in the next month.

Set both weekly and monthly progress goals.

This will allow you to monitor your progress over both the short-term and the longer-term. It also provides you with a way to "catch up" if you fall behind on any given week. As long as you're on target with your monthly goals, you're doing well. If you're consistently falling short of your goals, set smaller ones.

Sometimes Ph.D. students get so caught up in researching an idea or topic that they chase down all the tangents or references, even though this may have very little to do with their actual project. Remain aware of the limitations of your proposal – if you have a limited number of pages to devote to the literature review, it does not make sense to seek out hundreds of quotes or citations for it. Much of this will be wasted effort. By taking a few seconds to check in with yourself as you move through your tasks, you can be sure that you're focusing on the most salient or critical areas.

Try to accomplish no more than two to three tasks in each sitting. Try to make these tasks you have actively chosen to tackle, and make sure they are similar to each other.

It's a good idea to "chunk" or break down your goals into manageable, doable pieces. You can also maintain efficiency by grouping similar tasks together. Examples would be: making all necessary phone calls at one time, or spending one full day at the library, rather than making separate trips. Focusing on no more than two to three tasks ensures that you're not mentally shifting back and forth between different kinds of work, which can sometimes be confusing.

Set appropriate boundaries around your other responsibilities. Simplify your life, chores, and tasks wherever possible, so that you can leave enough time to work on your dissertation.

Very often, students decide that the dissertation year is a good time to lose weight, quit smoking, change bad habits, or take on many new responsibilities. Please don't do this to yourself. It's tempting, when everything is changing around us, to create even more change in our lives (possibly as a way to control *something*). This, however, can leave you feeling anxious and nervous, because people are built to handle only so much change at one time. If you must change some lifestyle habits or choices, do it slowly and easily. This will help you feel more comfortable, and is a more effective way to make your new habits "stick."

SECTION II: MOTIVATION

Motivation is a very important aspect of completing your dissertation. Most often, people have a great deal of energy when they begin this major project, but the energy begins to drain away as time goes on and life interferes. The tips in this section focus on helping you create and maintain positive motivation from the beginning to the end of your dissertation.

Realize that the dissertation is a choice. You can always choose something else.

This tip can be helpful when you feel that someone is "forcing" you to write the dissertation. None of us likes to be "forced" to do things, so an important aspect of staying motivated is realizing that you are choosing to do this as part of your life plan.

Bonus Exercise:

List all the ways your life will be better for having completed the dissertation. Post this list where you can see it every day. It may include items such as, "I'll never have to write another paper again," or "I'll get out into the real world," or… Well, you get the idea. Just make sure you list items that really excite you. You'll come to see the dissertation as one step on the journey. Connect to the exciting possibilities of the future.

Work on your dissertation at least ten minutes per day.

One of the suggestions my clients find most helpful is to work on their dissertations at least ten minutes each day. This has proven to be especially important for people who are working full-time and have trouble finding time. Even completing a ten-minute chunk of work can go a long way to keeping your self- talk positive. Try it for a week. Track how it feels. Instead of thinking, "I should work on it," you actually ARE working on it!

If you can't get started, try working for five minutes. Then stop.

This idea is for those days when your whole body and soul is resisting the dissertation. Your mind is saying, "You should do this," and "You should do that," and "How did you get so far behind?" and "You'll never finish," but your body and heart are saying, "I just can't. I just can't. It's too <overwhelming, scary, upsetting.> I just can't." Ever had one of those days? When you have a day like this, set a timer for five minutes and work for just that amount of time. After five minutes, stop.

This will "prime" you to begin work again the next day.
The idea is to leave yourself *wanting* to do more work,
rather than being *pushed* to do more work.

Bonus Tip:

Sometimes five-minute chunks are too long. In that case,
try one minute. It is also good if you can reward yourself
after accomplishing this – associate the dissertation work
with something positive!

Reward yourself along the way.

Too often, our motivation begins to lag because we're
doing too much work and not having enough fun. Often,
students feel as if they have to work non-stop, which,
unfortunately, actually makes you LESS productive. To
avoid falling into this trap, reward your progress along
the way.

Bonus Exercise:

Make a list of thirty inexpensive, simple experiences
you love (a serving of dessert, a walk in nature,
listening to music, reading a magazine, buying flowers),
and strive to enjoy at least three of these experiences

each week. You'll notice an amazing, positive difference in your energy and out- look.

Stay in close contact with your advisors –don't let fear or anxiety stall you.

This tip is really important because worrying about contacting your advisors can be one of the biggest drains on your energy and motivation. You know you have to send your advisor a product, but you're not quite done, so you put it off, and then you miss the dead- line, and then you feel bad, and then you avoid contacting him/her, and you start to feel drained by the stress! You're caught between wanting to turn in something, but dreading actually turning it in. You can avoid this by sending brief, monthly updates to stay in touch. These can be two-line emails saying, "Hi, I'm still working – hope you're well, will send product soon." Or something similar. Don't drain your motivation on this!

Bonus Exercise:

If you haven't contacted your advisor in a month or more, do it now. Put the book down and come back once you've accomplished this.

Work on the dissertation first thing in the morning –

get it out of the way.

Another good trick to stay motivated is to work on your dissertation first thing in the morning. Get up a few minutes early, block the time from distractions or interruptions, and get to work! You'll feel great, knowing that you've accomplished something important in the first twenty minutes of the day.

Bonus Tip:

If you have a laptop, keep it by your bed so you can work on the dissertation first thing in the morning. Progress is about consistency.

Keep a running "to do" list for dissertation–this will help you get back into it more easily.

One of the major complaints I hear is that it's difficult to get back into the dissertation at each sitting. One way to address this is to keep a running "to do" list of what you'll work on next. By referring to the list, you can get started immediately.

Bonus Tip:

Consider reviewing this list the night before, so you're ready to jump in first thing the next day

If you get stuck, change your environment–walk around or look at something new.

One of the best ways to get "unstuck" is to move your body or shift your experience. If you can't make the "perfect" words come, stop trying. You'll save yourself tons of frustration. Instead, go for a walk, wander around your space, do something different. We're much more receptive to ideas when we allow them in, rather than forcing them to come. Exercise is particularly good for clearing away obstacles when you're stuck.

Think of this as a marathon, not a wind sprint.

Most students treat the dissertation as a wind sprint, not a marathon. This means that they work extremely long hours at the beginning, throw their lives out of whack, push themselves until they "crash," and then can't get back to work after this. If you can see this process as a marathon, you'll know that you need to keep a steady and even pace to finish!

Track your progress visually.

It can be very helpful to keep a visual map of your dissertation progress. One of my clients did this by obtaining a map of the United States, along with a packet of push pins. He calculated that to complete his proposal, it would take him a certain number of hours, which he converted into "miles" for a driving trip across the US. Each day that he worked on his dissertation, he would move the push pin a little bit farther down the road. This helped him visually track his progress, and also injected a bit of lightness and humor into the intensity of the dissertation process. Have some fun with it!

Focus on your plans and life during and after the dissertation.

When you're in the dissertation process, it's tough to think about much else. However, it is important to make sure you're meeting your other "life" goals while working on this major project. Your motivation will stay high if you have close relationships, good physical energy, and feel as if your life is progressing satisfactorily, even if the emphasis is still on the dissertation. Keep it simple, but don't deny the pleasures in your life!

Stay connected to the past and the future.

It's important during the dissertation process to stay

"hooked in" to your social supports (family, relatives, childhood/college/grad school friends), as well as being open to new possibilities. Many of you will move away from your campus during the dissertation year, and you'll do well if you can build a life for yourself in your new setting while making progress on the dissertation. We all need other people, and we all need to feel connected, so allow yourself to meet new people, try new activities, take up new hobbies, or do the same old things in a new way.

Doing this will help the dissertation stay in its proper place – as one part of your life, not your whole life.

Plan for a HUGE treat after your defense–a week-long vacation or other reward.

This may go without saying, but you should definitely plan a huge vacation, treat, gift – something – for yourself after the defense. Create a timeline to the defense (See Section I: Planning/Goal Setting), as well as the Appendix for hints on creating this timeline), and plan a HUGE, amazing reward for your- self at this date. Focusing on a reward will often increase your motivation to meet dead- lines.

Create variety in your dissertation work – give yourself a chance to try new approaches, new ideas, and new techniques.

This will keep your energy and enthusiasm high. Allow yourself to try new technology, new ideas, and new ways of thinking. Allow yourself to think "out of the box" or to temporarily "break the mold," and notice how your energy rises.

Bonus Tip:

If you feel really, really low or just can't even begin – make it fun! Take a sheet of paper and write the problem in the center of the page. Write the question to be answered. Then fill in the space around it with possible solutions. Don't censor yourself – let the ideas flow. For example, the problem might be, "I can't stand the thought of working on my dissertation. I don't want to do it." The question to write down would therefore be: "How can I avoid working on my dissertation?" Some possible answers could be: "I could just not do it. I could run away. I could move out of state. I could work at McDonald's instead. I could become a cowboy." Allow yourself to consider ALL the possibilities. Do this until you have nothing left to say.

Then check your energy. See if this process helped "clear you" of your negativity.

Do one thing each day that makes your life better for you.

Aside from the dissertation, this is a good life practice. This tip refers to taking care of yourself, every day, even in "small ways". It's about improving your life, incrementally, day by day. So, for example, if there are things in your apartment which are broken or peeling or in need of repair, get them taken care of. Things in need of repair drain our energy and can make us feel low. Take one step each day to improve the quality of your life.

Bonus Tip:

Stop putting this off. Do it now. Life will be much easier if you practice taking care of problems as they arise rather than waiting for them to grow. This does not apply to "creating work" out of nothing as a procrastination strategy, however.

SECTION III: SELF-CARE

Establish good self-care habits *before* starting the dissertation.

Although it's never too late to start taking care of yourself, it's best if you can get some good habits in place *before* starting the dissertation process. This can include eating better, exercising more, practicing relaxation or meditation daily, and making time for friends, family, and fun. The stronger your self-care foundation, the easier the dissertation will be.

Bonus Tip: If you need to make some improvements in your self-care, tackle one area at a time. It takes about three weeks for something to become a habit, so make sure whatever you decide to do is something you can stick to for twenty-one consecutive days. This may also help you to keep your goals reasonable.

Balance the dissertation with other activities.

What if I told you that I had a job for you? In this job, you can work whenever you want, but you have to work more than twelve hours per day. You can't take breaks, and if you do, you have to worry about the job during those breaks. You'll most likely work almost entirely alone, and will have to set your own goals and rewards for progress. Your supervisors may or may not be supportive of you, or available when you need them. You'll likely be lonely, isolated, and feel anxious and worried. And there is no guarantee that your product will be accepted as is, anyway.

Would you want this kind of job? I hope not! Yet this is precisely the "job description" many Ph.D. students write for their dissertation process. Instead, I'd like to suggest that you practice balancing the dissertation work with other life activities – especially for those people who are not married and have no children. Single graduate students are the most prone to working non-stop on the dissertation, to the detriment of other facets of their lives. It's about balance – which is a good skill to learn for life, too.

Take extra care of yourself if you're far away from your school.

Many students move to new cities or towns for the dissertation year. If you are in this situation, please make extra sure that you stay connected to people in your life and don't isolate yourself. It's a good idea, when you move to a new town, to join a community gym, a local arts and crafts class, or the local library as a way of interacting with people. Solitude is fine, but it can become overwhelming when there is too much of it.

Keep your self-talk positive; actively com- bat negative self-talk.

"Self-Talk" is that "voice" in your head that gives you comments and feedback on yourself. It can be positive, such as "You're doing great!" or "You look terrific today!", but unfortunately, most of our self-talk is extremely negative and critical, more like, "That was stupid" or "I can't believe you said that" or "Now they know you're dumb."

The important thing to remember is that negative self-talk is NOT TRUE. No matter how reasonable it sounds, or how calm and rational its approach, it's always designed to keep you feeling bad. In coaching, we call this negative critical voice "The Gremlin." Practice "locking your Gremlin up." Don't let him or her come out to play.

Protect your energy.

This is a really important concept because it gives you an

inner compass – internal guidance on who you are and what you want to do. I'd like you to practice becoming aware of your energy throughout the day, noting when you feel really good and positive, and when you feel sad or negative. If you observe your energy closely, you'll notice that certain activities give you energy (talking to your friends, reading a good book, having quiet time) and others drain you (constant background noise, the evening news). Strive to protect your energy. Plug the drains.

Bonus Exercise:

Spend one whole day observing your energy. Notice how you feel at various points throughout your day. Graph your high and low points. This will help you identify energy boosters and your natural rhythms.

Double Bonus Exercise:

Plug one energy drain today.

Schedule a complete "day off" from the dissertation at least twice a month.

Breaks are important to keep your enthusiasm and energy high. Allow yourself to take breaks from the dissertation and the process at least twice each month.

Schedule these about three weeks in advance, and protect this time. Instead of worrying or fretting or pushing yourself, spend this day reconnecting with yourself, nature, or people you care for. You'll feel an amazing difference.

Know about your natural rhythms – work with them, not against them.

Your natural body rhythms are an important clue in finding the best schedule for working on your dissertation. If you are a morning person, it might be best to get up early and work on the dissertation first thing. If you are more of a night person, it will probably be best to work on the dissertation in the evening (though you run a somewhat higher risk of being "too tired" or otherwise putting it off). Most people have a natural decline in energy between three and four o'clock in the afternoon. Plan your study and work time accordingly.

Treat yourself as well as you can.

Have strong boundaries, keep your word, eat well, sleep well, and play well. Treat your- self like your best asset – because you are! It sounds simple. And it is! These simple actions can make a huge difference in your health, outlook, and attitude.

Make the dissertation part of a good life!

Incorporate the dissertation into the rhythm and flow of your life. The same way you make time to brush your teeth each day, to sleep, to shower, etc., make time to work on the dissertation. This also means that you allow yourself to take part in activities that make you feel good. Many of my clients initially resist this, feeling afraid that they won't "ever" get back to the dissertation if they allow themselves to feel good. If you can trust in yourself and do something enjoyable, you'll actually get back to the dissertation much sooner!

It won't be painless. Don't make it overly painful.

Please! Don't make the dissertation more difficult than it has to be. Don't take on too big of a project, too much work, or too many outside responsibilities. Practice doing things the easy way. This will make the process much smoother.

Bonus Exercise:

Identify one area in which you've been approaching the dissertation the "hard" way. Identify and implement a better strategy. Hint: Sometimes this might involve asking for help.

Protect your time and investment in the dissertation process.

Remember, the dissertation is YOUR project for YOUR degree. Keep track of how much you're working and protect your time. Sometimes, advisors want to add extra work to your project, which may delay your plans for graduation. Practice maintaining your boundaries in this area. You have the right to negotiate for your timeline to complete your degree.

Respect important events.

This tip comes from my own experience. During my dissertation year, I was invited to my friend Mary's wedding. We had met during my Master's program and had stayed in semi-close touch for a few years after. When I received the invitation, I felt that I was too busy and couldn't possibly take time away from my dissertation to be a bridesmaid and have some fun. Mary never spoke to me again. Perhaps there were other reasons, but I suspect that they were related to my refusal to make room in my dissertation process for her. In a year-long process, would taking a weekend off have been such a big deal? Probably not. Hindsight is 20/20.

Work no more than six days a week. Give yourself time off at least one, preferably two days, per week.

This is especially important for students who work full-time while completing their degree. Your body needs time "off" from thinking, working, planning, and studying, to relax and recuperate. Structure your life so you have enough time to take time off. This may involve simplifying your life. Do it.

Keep a journal or engage in some other self-reflective activity – use this as a place to record any fears, worries, etc. Get them out of your mind and out of your way.

The dissertation process is filled with many worries, fear, and anxiety. It can help to write out those negative feelings and get them out of your mind and out of your way. Just the process of writing them out clears your mind and can help you work on new solutions. It also clears out your negativity.

Bonus Tip:

If you would like to journal, but don't know what to

say, start with writing about not knowing what to say.

If you feel stressed, angry, or depressed most of the time, recognize that this is a problem. Allow yourself to seek appropriate professional help.

The dissertation process is a stressful time. If you feel that you are having trouble coping with the demands, for whatever reason, allow yourself to ask for and accept professional help. There are no extra points for doing this alone.

SECTION IV: TIME MANAGEMENT

You do have time for the dissertation. You just need to make it a priority.

A common theme in our society is being "too busy" to implement certain habits or skills. I challenge this by saying that we all have the same amount of time in each day or week. Some people choose to place their priorities on activities other than the dissertation. However, if you make the dissertation a main priority each week, in much the same way you would show up for a part-time job or other commitment, you will complete it sooner.

Work expands to fill the time allotted to it. This is Parkinson's Law.

Allot less time to a particular task. You'll get more done. Two hours of solid progress is much better than four hours of "so-so" progress.

If you travel a lot, for work or other reasons, consider investing in a laptop.

You can get an incredible amount of work done when you're on a plane or train.

Save tasks like revising or editing for spare moments in the day.

If you work full-time, but have a ten-minute break at lunch, you can begin to make notes about revisions or edits.

Build the dissertation into your day as much as possible.

Integrating the dissertation into your daily life is a fantastic habit. It is much more helpful than placing the work in its own category, where it begins to become an overwhelming and daunting task.

For some people, it may be best to work on the dissertation once per week.

Schedule this time first, and hold to it strictly. It is an appointment with yourself. You're important. Don't break it.

Treat the dissertation like a part-time job – not your whole life.

Even if you were working in academia, you'd put your work down sometimes! You'd also need to be more efficient and able to juggle various tasks. I work with my clients to help them make between two and six hours of solid progress each week. Then I ask them to go out and do other things!

Remember that it's YOUR dissertation.

Keep track of the work you want to accomplish and what you want to create. Some faculty members forget that you have to move on to life after graduate school, and therefore can't afford to keep the dissertation as an open issue for years. If you have selected a committee you can work well with, you should feel comfortable delimiting and defining the scope of your work into something that is doable and works for you.

Write down your favorite ways to procrastinate. Monitor your behavior against this list.

Keeping track of your favorite ways to procrastinate will help attune you to those times when you are, indeed, procrastinating. These moments are very different from taking planned, legitimate breaks. Some good hints that you ARE procrastinating: you find your- self doing activities you don't like, just to avoid working on the dissertation. You tackle huge, parallel projects, with little planning or forethought. You think about the dissertation a lot, but "never get around to it."

Don't take on too many new projects during the dissertation year.

It is important to limit the number of new responsibilities you take on during this year. The main priorities should be self-care, maintaining your quality of life, and the dissertation. You will be able to make great professional strides and a great deal of other progress once you have your degree. Keep your eyes on the prize.

Do what you say, and say what you do.

If your dissertation is important to you, act like it. If you've done a good job, say so. If you could have done better, acknowledge this. Keep looking forward and moving on. Act and speak consistently.

Do the worst things first. This will save you worry and anxiety and get them over with.

Quite often, we delay dealing with the "worst" things. This causes them to become more worrying and troublesome. I recommend that you tackle the worst jobs first. This will rebalance your energy.

If you get stuck for more than a month, and haven't worked on your dissertation at all, take BIG action.

Get a support group, get a coach, do some- thing. If you had cut your finger, you'd (hope- fully) clean and bandage it. You wouldn't just let it keep bleeding and wait to see what happened. Getting stuck in the dissertation is the same thing. When you first see yourself getting stuck and feeling bad, prevent it from going any further.

Don't put your life on total "hold" while you work on the dissertation.

Life has a funny way of moving along, whether we're ready or not. The task is not to avoid everything but work on the dissertation. I think, instead, the key is to find a way to balance the dissertation with your other life demands and life goals. The major lesson is to consistently achieve at a high level, with minimum time and effort. It can be done.

KNOW that you CAN do this. It's not "if," it's "when."

By now, you've written numerous papers, read extensively, and have most likely met many major goals in your academic journey. You will meet this one as well!

SECTION V: WORK SPACE/WORK HABITS

Create a comfortable and efficient work- space for yourself.

At a minimum, this should include a large writing surface, nearby shelves and surfaces to hold materials, room for your computer and printer, good lighting, and a complete supply of office materials.

Keep your work environment clean, pleasing, and free of distractions.

It's very helpful to have extra room to work in. Make it a habit to "clear out" your work space on a weekly or monthly basis, filing away articles or information you aren't actively using, shelving books, etc. This will keep your mind clear and focused.

Bonus Tip:

Sometimes, just cleaning out your space is enough to get you started working when you're stuck.

Make sure that your office arrangement is ergonomically correct.

Ensure that your desk and chair are at the correct height, and your computer monitor and keyboard are arranged appropriately.

Have a light source above your computer screen – this will decrease eyestrain. Place a chair mat under your chair – this makes it easier to move around the office without straining your back or legs. It's important to be comfortable!

Get into the habit of copying or "backing up" your material each week.

Pick one day a week to do this. Backing up is important to prevent unnecessary loss of data. It's simple to set up, and only takes a few minutes to do, so get in the habit of weekly backups. Consider backing up each day if you've completed a great deal of analysis or other statistical computations.

Stock your office with relevant manuals, materials, and reference texts.

Keep these in plain view and nearby. You will refer to them often and don't want to waste time looking for them.

Keep an extra printer cartridge and some extra office supplies on hand.

Your printer is very likely to run out of ink just when you're printing the proposal or final draft. This happened to me, and it was after midnight, and all the office supply stores were closed!

Have all information well organized, clearly filed, and accessible.

One of the first tasks I ask my clients to complete is a thorough organization and filing of their dissertation materials. There is not much worse than digging through a huge file box of articles, trying to find that one perfect quote. If you don't know where to start, start by getting organized.

Create a "catch all" file to keep track of thoughts, notes, and leads that don't fit any- where else.

This is a great place to keep track of all those "odds and ends" that you might use, or would like to use, but don't know exactly where to fit them. It's also a good place to keep notes you've jotted down or vague ideas you'd like to explore further. Sort through this folder periodically – you'll be amazed by some of the insights you'll gain or the connections you'll make. The other benefit of this type of file is that you can jot down ideas or thoughts to clear them out of your head, but also be able to find them when you need them.

Allow at least ten minutes to make the transition between activities.

Be sure to give yourself time to make the mental shift into, and out of, working on your dissertation. You might spend the first ten minutes looking over the notes you made when you last stopped working. Also, give yourself ten minutes at the end of your work time so that you can make a smooth transition into your next task.

Limit the time you spend checking email or surfing the Internet.

Save this for breaks, or as a "reward" for completing a task. Research has shown that people who spend a great deal of time surfing the Internet are more likely to be depressed and anxious than those who don't spend as much time on the Net. Too much Internet time also reduces your motivation and productivity.

Hold your dissertation work time as sacred. Allow calls to go directly to the answering machine, as call

"screening" can be a distraction and an interruption.

Some of my clients create dissertation time, but then "screen" their phone calls. This is a distraction – each time the phone rings, your attention shifts as you listen to your callers leaving messages. You're likely to work best if you can allow your calls to go silently to voicemail. Consider turning your phone's ringer off, and replacing the silence with instrumental or classical music, playing low in the background. This will decrease the disconcerting effect of that slightly spooky overly quiet silence that can surround the dissertation work.

Make sure your computer is up-to-date and able to handle your data, files, etc. with ease. If you're not very computer-savvy, develop a relationship with someone who is – you may need their skills!

My computer "died" in the middle of my dissertation process, with the information still on the hard drive. (No backups.) This was not good.

Make notes to yourself about where you've stopped in a particular task or project, and how you need to begin in the next session.

This will cut down on fumbling around and figuring out what to do next, saving you time and increasing productivity.

Take a break every twenty to thirty minutes to stand up, walk around, and get some blood flowing. Take regular stretch breaks, too.

Be aware of your body's need for movement, food, water, and rest. Get into a regular habit of stretching your fingers and wrists, flexing your feet and legs (this prevents blood from pooling in your lower body), and giving yourself scalp and neck massages.

Make the most effective use of the technology that is available to you.

Advancements such as voice recognition software, faxing from your computer, and high speed Internet connections (for down- loading programs and information) can make your life much easier. Use them to the maxi- mum extent you are comfortable.

SECTION VI: MOMENTUM BUILDING / CLEARING BLOCKS

Look for the easy way.

Make the dissertation as easy as possible, and make your choices based on what feels the easiest. Too often, students select unwieldy topics, incredibly complex study designs, and generally make their lives much more difficult than necessary. Save your writing and research masterpieces for after graduation.

Realize that the dissertation is NOT your life's masterpiece.

The best dissertation is a finished dissertation. The dissertation is really just one more project; a long research paper to complete, in a series of research papers you have already written. You WILL create more wonderful articles and more elegant research designs. Save these for when you're out of school and getting paid for it.

Remember, momentum is the key.

Momentum is built by small actions, applied

consistently – a body in motion tends to stay in motion. Always stay open to working on your dissertation in small pieces, and small chunks of time. Integrate it into your life.

Take small, baby steps.

One way to generate momentum is to begin by taking small steps, each day, to bring you closer to a completed dissertation. Rather than large, grand plans that often remain unfinished, set teeny tiny goals: "I will write two sentences before breakfast." "I will make that phone call during my lunch break." Anything. Remember, "The longest journey begins with a single step."

Save revision or editing for certain days.

Keep "clean up" tasks (footnoting, format- ting, etc.) for those days when you want to accomplish something on your dissertation, but don't feel energetic enough to generate new material. (I found that typing my bibliography in proper APA style was just perfect for those mindless days!)

Use concept/mind mapping to get unstuck.

Mind mapping is a technique for quickly generating ideas and possible pathways to explore an idea. It allows you to create a visual progression of your topic or idea, which can then be converted to a linear outline to aid in writing. See Section III: Boosting Creativity for a greater explanation of this technique.

If you find yourself getting overwhelmed trying to conceptualize your topic, try to explain it to someone else.

This can clear your blocks or reveal where you need more information. Your listener may also ask thought-provoking questions to help you move forward.

Don't be afraid to change your location or study venue if you get stuck.

You can read articles at the gym, at a coffee bar, outside on the porch – not everything has to occur in the library!

Slow and steady wins the race.

Don't burn yourself out too early. (Remember the marathon!) While it is fine, and sometimes necessary, to expend tremendous energy to complete a task, it is not an effective long-term strategy for the dissertation.

If you get stuck while writing, ask yourself, "What is my point here?" and then ask, "How can I most easily make

my point?"

Sometimes, revisiting your main purpose or "point" can help you clarify and simplify your ideas.

Break each chapter down into smaller "term paper" type chunks.

This may decrease your feelings of being overwhelmed, and help you gauge your progress.

Write the introduction last.

I have heard of, and worked with, clients who could not begin the substantive chapters because they were not able to complete the introduction. They labored over the introduction for months, trying to articulate where they were going to go in the paper before having written the paper. I would strongly suggest that you begin by writing the substantive chapters, and save the introduction for last. It's easier to write about where you're going to go after you've already been there.

If you can write one page a day, you will have written more than twenty pages in a month. For most people, this represents about one half to one third of a chapter. This means that in eight to ten months, you could have the entire paper written.

This is a way of framing what is reasonable to accomplish. Too often, students labor for days and days over one page. This is too slow. Do whatever you need to do to move faster. This tip also reinforces the importance of completing seemingly small actions each day, as they can add up very quickly.

If all else fails, clean out your closet or do some exercise. Both of these activities are marvelous for shifting your perspective.

This may sound funny, but again, it's about moving the energy around and getting "unstuck."

Consider all "setbacks" or "mistakes" as only temporary.

In my practice, I call this, "Never take No for an answer." There are always options and solutions for overcoming stalls or setbacks. Don't take comments like "It can't be done," or "There's no way to do this" seriously. Maintain a positive outlook and attitude – you can overcome *any* and *all* stumbling blocks.

SECTION VII: BOOSTING CREATIVITY

If you're really stuck, get moving.

Moving your body (exercising, dancing, going for a walk around the neighborhood) will get you unstuck, while boosting your physical fitness!

Try having an "Opposite Day."

This day is one in which you do everything oppositely from the moment you wake up – you get up on the other side of the bed, brush your teeth with your other hand, maybe even eat dinner for breakfast. Sounds a little odd, perhaps, but it's great for getting unstuck.

Switch to something else for a while – don't force it.

If you've been working with an idea for some time and just can't get it to fit, give yourself a break from it and move on to some- thing else. You will likely come up with the answer or framework when you turn your attention to something else.

Allow time for ideas to coalesce – rhythmic activities give your brain the chance to play around and incubate ideas.

If you're working to organize a great deal of information, one of the best ways to do this is to become involved in some rhythmical activity which allows your mind to wander and explore the options. Examples of such activities might be walking, running, swimming, cycling, chopping vegetables, sewing, or driving – anything that you can do without needing words.

Be creative in other ways – cooking, art, a new way to work or school.

The more creative you are in your daily life, the more creatively you will write. This is probably due to a greater number of experiences, a different way of experiencing, and allowing yourself to have fun.

Do an activity you loved in childhood – baking cookies, finger-painting, anything.

One of the activities I recommend to my clients is to revisit activities they loved as children. I ask that they schedule "play days" every few weeks, when they put all seriousness aside and just have fun. This has done wonders for improving their attitude, out- look, and approach to the dissertation.

Argue for the "other side" in your work (i.e., support

the alternate opinion).

If you're stuck in developing an argument, consider playing "devil's advocate" and writing or arguing for the "other side." This can sharpen your thinking and analysis and help you combine additional information to make the strongest possible argument.

Bonus Tip:

Consider the power of "What If". You can use the idea "What If?" as a way to solidify important ideas. Ask yourself "What If?" this wasn't true, or "What If?" this didn't happen- this can give you a new sense of mastery over your theoretical arguments.

Use art supplies, colored markers, and colored paper to jazz up the research process.

I used to keep my project notes on colored index cards – sometimes written in colored ink – and I printed various drafts of my dissertation on colored paper (which also helped me to better organize them). Use whatever method appeals to you to make the dissertation process less dreary and boring.

If you're not sure how to proceed, try story- boarding or mind mapping.

These are two visual techniques that can help you develop your ideas. In storyboarding, you tape several pieces of paper up on the wall. On the last piece of paper, you write where you want to go (the goal, argument, or end point). On the other pieces of paper, you write the steps you need to lead up to that argument or conclusion. This will help you to see the gaps in your current knowledge and enable you to find possible pathways to proceed.

In mind mapping, you take a piece of paper and write the central concept or theme in the middle of the page. You then draw spokes radiating from this central concept to all the possible topic areas. You can then develop each topic area further.

Both techniques are ways of loosening up your thinking and allowing you to see new links and associations.

Bonus Tip:

One excellent, and relatively inexpensive, mind mapping program I use is Inspiration 6.0. It is available from http://www.inspiration.com, and there is a free download you can try for thirty days to see if it is right for you.

If you're stuck in the writing, sit down and just allow the words to flow.

Using this "stream of consciousness" approach for at least three pages will help get you unstuck.

If you're stuck for an idea of how to proceed, one of my advisors suggested this: open the dictionary to any page. Choose a word. Figure out how your dissertation topic relates to this word. This should get those juices flowing!

Bonus Tip:

Another exercise you can try is to take a piece of paper and write the problem across the top of the page. Then list the letters of the alphabet in a column down the left-hand side of the page (A...B...C... all the way to Z). Then, take each letter and write down a solution (no matter how strange) that might answer the question or solve the problem. For example, let's say that your problem is that you don't know how to develop the analysis for your research. You might come up with a list like this: A: Ask for help. B: Buy a completed dissertation from someone and use it as my own (just for instance). C: Call my Mom. D: Decide to move to Kansas. You get the idea. If you do this quickly, without too much thinking or censoring, you will unlock some possibilities that will get you moving again.

The greatest creativity is found when you allow yourself the greatest freedom to work and rework your ideas.

Spend some time discussing your "stuckness" with a trusted friend or colleague.

Sometimes another person can provide perspective to get you moving.

Sleep on it.

Hold the idea or problem in your mind before you go to bed. Allow your subconscious to come up with the answer while you sleep.

Listen to classical music, especially Bach or Mozart (or anything similar).

Classical music has been shown to sharpen focus and increase concentration while unlocking creativity.

Think quantity. You'll get quality.

Research has shown that in looking for creative solutions, the more possibilities or options, the better. So if you're stuck on some- thing related to your dissertation, the more possible options you can come up with for solving the problem, the better your final solution will be.

SECTION VIII: GETTING SUPPORT

Don't be afraid to ask for help.

Many of my clients feel that they MUST do all the work for their dissertation without help. Even if they hate it. Or maybe ESPECIALLY if they hate it. I'm suggesting that there is a better way. Get help for all the tasks you don't like or aren't particularly good at. There are many resources for you to select from – coaches to help you set goals or make progress, editors to review your writing, statisticians to help you with your calculations, office assistants to help with data entry.

The main point is to keep moving forward, by whatever means necessary. There are no extra points for doing all the work by yourself.

The dissertation doesn't have to be a solitary process.

We often make it one, though. We hole up in our homes or the library, feeling stressed and overwhelmed in our solitude. Don't be afraid to access services designed to support you in this process.

Actively enlist the help of friends, neighbors, and

colleagues.

This is equally important whether you're living on your own, or with a spouse or children. Allow yourself to accept help when and where it is offered – or to ask for it if and when you need it! This can include getting help with data entry, with childcare, or with household chores. Allow people to help you now – you can always return the favor once your dissertation is completed.

Create a support group.

This group can comprise students from your program, or from other disciplines. Create some sort of weekly or monthly meeting as a space to share successes, discuss ideas, and try out job talks; anything you need.

Get a coach.

Hiring a coach is one of the most significant steps you can take to maximize your dissertation success. I have worked with clients who have been working on their dissertations, sometimes for many years – and they have completed their degrees within four to six months of beginning our work together. I know that other coaches have experienced similar successes. A coach is there for you, committed to your goals and your progress.

Utilize your departmental and university resources.

This sounds pretty self-evident, perhaps, but you might be surprised at how many resources your department or university has to support your progress. Some examples are grants or fellowships, editors, statisticians, access to specialized references, and interlibrary loans, just to name a few. Start looking!

Establish more contact, not less, with your Committee Chair.

Although this depends on the individual, it is usually best to have more contact, rather than less, with your Committee Chair. If you've chosen someone who is available and supportive, as recommended elsewhere in this book, you should feel comfortable asking questions or discussing various directions. This will save you from wasting time exploring pointless tangents, and having to redo sections at a later date. Staying in contact with your Chair may also provide you with information on new resources, departmental developments, and other resources that can affect your dissertation process.

Set up a "working date" with another student.

Many of my clients have reported this to be a helpful and effective means of making progress on their dissertations. They meet another student either at home or in the library or a coffee shop. Each student works on his or her own material, but in the company of someone else. This can be a wonderful and productive experience.

If both you and your significant other are in Ph.D. programs and working on the dissertation at the same time, consider "trading weeks" to work.

This technique has worked well for some of my clients. The way it works is this: you each agree to work two weeks per month on your dissertation. You can take two-week blocks, or alternate weeks. In a month with five weeks, you spend the fifth week together, catching up on your relationship. Alternatively, consider creating working dates with each other, and share the dissertation time each week.

For example: Joe and Mary are both in doctoral programs. Joe works on his dissertation for weeks one and two of the month. Mary works on her dissertation for weeks three and four of the month. In a month with five weeks, they each take that week "off" and spend time together. In weeks one and two of the month, Mary may do a bit more around the house- she may cook more often, or do errands more often. In weeks three and four, Joe may cook more often and do errands more often. Alternatively, Joe and Mary can both contribute equally to the household tasks, but then set up "working dates" a few times each week where they will spend time together, but each working on their own paper.

Bonus Tip:

This also works well if your partner has work to complete, even if it's not dissertation-related.

When you go away to visit friends or family, don't carry many dissertation materials with you.

Too often, you won't open them – and will only have a lot of extra weight to carry around. If you *must* take something along, consider taking a couple of articles or some pages to revise or edit.

Subscribe to the All But Dissertation Survival Guide.

This twice-monthly email newsletter is dedicated to helping doctoral students complete their dissertations. You can subscribe to the newsletter by pointing your browser to http://www.ecoach.com. There are also archives of past issues you can read through.

Only talk with others about the dissertation as much as is comfortable – for you and for them.

While it is important to seek support and understanding, sometimes students talk about nothing except their dissertations, making it difficult for them to maintain appropriate perspective. The dissertation is just one part of life. Take time to connect with people around other shared interests. This will be more satisfying and fulfilling than fretting over the dissertation in every conversation.

Don't play the "comparison" game. Everyone is different, and each student approaches the dissertation in his or her own way.

As much as possible, avoid the "comparison" game. Stay focused on your work, your game plan, and your progress.

Join email lists or news communities that support your work.

You can gain valuable contacts, information, insight, and support from these communities. One of my clients provided me with information on WRK4US, (www.woodrow.org/phd/WRK4US), an email discussion list devoted to doctoral students in the humanities.

Be supportive of yourself.

Take care of yourself, speak nicely to your- self, and take responsibility for meeting your needs. If you don't support yourself, it is difficult to accept support from other people.

SECTION IX: TALKING TO OTHERS ABOUT YOUR DISSERTATION

If anyone asks about your dissertation progress, always say it's going "GREAT."

This will help you avoid comments, criticism, and who knows – you may be motivated to make it a reality!

Monitor the level of competitiveness in your program and your social circle.

Try this test: If, after spending time with your colleagues, you feel anxious, annoyed, worried, or depressed, it is likely that there is a great deal of competitiveness in your group. Watch out for this, and allow yourself to take breaks from these meetings to keep your energy and motivation high.

Know that many people won't understand the process very well, if at all.

Many times, my clients are frustrated by the people in their lives asking, "When will you be finished?" and "What's taking so long just write the darn thing." You can try to explain your actions. But if this doesn't work,

recognize that it sometimes takes going through the
process to know what it's about.

**Use language that is as simple and clear as possible
when discussing your theories or process.**

The clearer you can be in speaking about it, the clearer
and easier it will be to write about and develop further.

**Stay in touch with colleagues who have completed your
program.**

This can help you to "keep your eyes on the prize" in
terms of the rewards and motivation for finishing. It's
also helpful to obtain first- hand knowledge and advice
from someone who has just completed the process.

Practice compartmentalizing your dissertation.

While integrating the dissertation into your life is
important, it's also important to know when it's time to
talk about other things. Remind yourself that there is
more to you, and your life, than just your dissertation!

SECTION X: BEATING PROCRASTINATION

Use the smallest possible amount of time to get you started.

This may mean spending as little as one to five minutes on your work, initially. You need to "retrain" your perceptions to realize that the dissertation isn't so bad, and that you actually *like* your work.

Use a system of rewards to break down your procrastination.

These don't have to be expensive, but they should be important and make you feel good. This is not the time to be upset with yourself for needing rewards. Use them and get your work done.

Make a distinction between true procrastination and the lull that comes while your ideas are coalescing.

When you're working to coherently organize large amounts of information and are unable to write, you are probably in the coalescing stage. If you haven't even started reading the material, it may be procrastination.

Work on something related to your dissertation at least three times per week.

Whether it is just filing some papers or ordering some materials, anything, no matter how small, will keep the dissertation in your thoughts and keep it from becoming a mysterious, looming unknown.

Try to identify the source of your procrastination. Is it fear? Is it exhaustion? Is it perfectionism?

Once you have identified the source, actively work to diminish these barriers. If you are afraid, try to find evidence indicating that you can be successful. If it's exhaustion, spend some time rethinking your priorities. If it's perfectionism, try to break this habit, slowly and surely. (See Section X: Letting Go of Perfectionism.)

Monitor what aspects of the dissertation are unpleasant for you. One main reason we procrastinate is that we don't like what we're doing.

If you dislike data entry, or feel bogged down by the details, consider asking for help. Trade tasks with a colleague, hire some assistance for a brief time, find a way to reframe or rework your task into something more pleas- ant. Are you procrastinating because working on your dissertation is a lonely task? Start working in public places, such as libraries and coffee houses. Once your needs are being met, you will no longer need to procrastinate.

Make certain your tasks don't feel too large or overwhelming. Remember to set small, manageable goals.

Sometimes we procrastinate because the task ahead feels too daunting. Find a balance between looking at the "big picture" and staying focused on your step-by-step progress. Continually ask yourself, "What is one thing I could do RIGHT NOW that would bring me closer to a completed dissertation?"

Allow yourself to "not know" and come back to it later.

Sometimes, while working on the dissertation, graduate students find that they don't know something, and then waste hours trying to track it down. I've had many clients describe "wild goose chases" in the library – they spend hours tracking down information, and later, realize this information is most useful only as a footnote.

Don't spend your time this way, as it will only

discourage you. When you come up against something you don't know, practice asking yourself, "Is knowing this absolutely crucial for me to proceed further?" If not, let it wait.

Keep small, easy projects for times when you're tired or burnt out, but want to keep making progress.

Typing the bibliography, creating your data tables, formatting, spellchecking, and the like, are all ways to continue working which are not that demanding.

Schedule daily rewards.

Start your day with something enjoyable, and end your day with something enjoyable. You'll feel better, be taking good care of yourself, and won't need to procrastinate, because your needs will be met.

Allow the dissertation process to be as easy as possible.

Writing your dissertation might not be pain- less, but try not to make it more painful than it needs to be. Like any other project in your life, it will get done if you work consistently towards it. I ask my clients to keep in mind the words, "easy and done," which they may repeat when they feel the project or process is becoming too difficult. Try using this phrase when you feel worried or negative about your work. It may help you move back into it more easily.

Limit the amount of time you spend watching television or surfing the Internet.

It's probably not a surprise that these are the two largest time wasters in our modern world. If there are certain TV shows you love to watch, consider taping them and watching the tapes as a reward for working. Also, limit email checking to no more than two or three times per day. Except for urgent emails, hold off on replying until you have completed your work for that day. Also, turn off the ringer on your phone, and don't "screen" your calls. The world can wait for a few hours.

Try to work on the dissertation whenever you think of it.

Much of the time, we think of working on the dissertation at odd times throughout the day – perhaps when we're involved in other activities. At these times, it is very helpful if you can do one small thing for your dissertation, rather than waiting until you have a big block of uninterrupted time.

Create a list of easy, but important, dissertation "to

dos" and keep it with you.

Use spare moments such as time on the bus, waiting for the doctor, or waiting in line to create a plan for tackling the items on your list. One of the main goals of this exercise is to integrate the dissertation into your daily life as much as possible.

Consider working on the "worst things" first.

If you're dreading getting started, (as Nike says) "Just Do It!" Get the worst items cleared out so you can be free of them.

Be supportive of yourself. You wouldn't be procrastinating if you could help it!

Remember that you are doing the best you can. Use the strategies in this book to the best of your ability, and tell that inner, critical voice to "shut up."

SECTION XI: LETTING GO OF PERFECTIONISM

Learn to recognize feelings of anxiety or depression as indicators of perfectionism.

When you are feeling anxious or depressed about your work, it is a good sign that perfectionism is present. When you feel anxious or sad about your work, explore why this is so. If you feel as though your work is never good enough, consciously rework these negative messages. They are self-defeating and unhelpful.

Burnout and exhaustion are other signs of perfectionism.

If you're feeling exhausted or burnt out, this is a sign that you're trying to do too many things, TOO well. Work to simplify your life wherever possible. Get help with this if necessary.

Avoid "all or nothing" or "black or white"thinking about your dissertation.

"My dissertation will never be done if I don't spend eighteen hours a day on it." "I have to read *everything* ever written in order to make this good enough." No statement that has the words "always," "never," "should," or "ever" can possibly be true – these are good "watchwords" for "all or nothing" thinking.

Practice allowing yourself to be less than perfect.

Students who are perfectionist about the dissertation often have extremely high standards in other areas of their lives. Practice living a life that isn't rigidly perfect. Don't make the bed one day, leave the dishes in the sink overnight – realize that the world won't end if you give less than 110% effort.

Reframe "failure" as the guidepost to success. All feedback moves you closer to being finished with your dissertation.

The sooner you realize what is the "wrong way," you're that much closer to finding the "right way." We all make mistakes or have stumbling blocks in our progress. The most successful people learn from them and let them go. A great example is of Thomas Edison, who had 5000 failures before inventing the light bulb on the 5001st try.

Loosen your hold on high expectations.

Allow yourself to try, not win. Allow your- self to have

fun – focus on the process, not only on the quality of the output.

Monitor feelings of jealousy, envy, and competition.

Some students matriculate in extremely competitive and envy-filled programs. If you find that you've become more critical of your- self and others, look at the people you are spending time with. If you spend time criticizing others, you will feel more pressure to prove that you're "better" than them, thereby cementing your perfectionism even further.

More of everything is not always better.

Many perfectionists behave as if extra work, extra time, and extra energy always result in higher quality output. This is not always the case. Learn to find a balance between working hard and working smart.

Know that perfectionism is often driven by the desire to be accepted and loved.

Take a look at yourself and your life and find places where you don't feel adequately accepted or loved. Take the necessary steps to obtain the support you need – a mentor, coach, therapist, or close friend can help you meet this need and stop it from being such a huge focus in your life.

Relax! Learn to lighten up!

Bring more simple joy into your life. Take walks. Spend time with your pet or a small child. Read a book. Watch a comedy. These activities, when done consistently, will help you create a place of inner joy that is not based on the attitudes of other people.

Life is meant to be joyful. If it's not joyful, it's not living.

Let go of the past.

Quite often, people who struggle with perfectionism have trouble letting go of past mistakes or events. They tend to carry around a lot of guilt about things they did, things they didn't do, things they thought of doing but didn't, things they didn't think of doing and didn't, things. Well, you get the idea. Practice living in this moment, here and now.

Learn to say No. Practice often.

Don't overload yourself with more work or responsibilities when you are trying to deal with perfectionism. I used to take on far too many tasks so that I could be liked, admired, and accepted. I spent too many nights working late into the night, earning praise from others, but feeling tired and empty and run down inside. I eventually recognized and dealt with my perfectionism, and now live a life that is much more focused on what I want and need, rather than what I can do to impress others.

Keep track of what's most important to you. Keep your life simple.

Often, people struggling with perfectionism have difficulty setting appropriate boundaries. They take on too much work, try hard to be accepted, and lose track of their priori- ties in the process. During the dissertation year, your two main goals are to complete the dissertation and do the minimum required to run your life. Keep these as your two main tasks.

If you keep doing the same old things the same old way, you'll always get what you've always gotten.

The hallmark of a successful person is that he or she uses feedback to modify and shape his or her behavior for more successful out- comes. People who are perfectionist tend to adhere rigidly to certain standards, *regardless* of the task at hand. Practice prioritizing. Realize that some things really are more important than others – not everything has to be done with the same level of detail or attention. Try not to keep beating your head against the same old wall.

Redefine perfect.

Perfectionism means different things to different people. I like to think of perfect as related to doing my best, at all times, with every- thing I know and have at that moment. If you apply this to your dissertation process, and know that you, too, are doing the best you can with what you have, perhaps you will find that you have attained perfection, and won't need to keep ceaselessly striving for it.

SECTION XII: MANAGING ANXIETY

Practice diaphragmatic breathing regularly, especially when you feel anxious.

Diaphragmatic breathing is a form of deep breathing which is linked to increased feelings of calmness and relaxation. Focus on taking breaths that are centered in your midsection – around the level of your belly button. Focus on having your abdomen push out when you take a breath in. Do this five to eight times to help calm and center yourself.

Reframe the anxiety as something positive.

Anxiety is a sign that you're moving out of your comfort zone – stretching into a new place of growth and excitement. So take the perspective that the anxiety shows that you're moving and growing. It's not something to be feared, it's something that's helping you move closer to who you really are and what you want to be.

If your anxiety is overwhelming or debilitating, seek professional help immediately.

Sometimes you feel anxious and worried and helpless

and stuck – and this feeling doesn't get better and it doesn't go away. If this describes you, please seek professional help immediately. You don't have to live this way! A mental health professional can provide you with information, skills, and coping strategies to help you work through your anxiety.

Get moving!

When you feel anxious, one of the best things you can do is move your body. Take a quick walk around the neighborhood, go to the gym, anything! Exercise releases chemicals that make you feel good, and demands full diaphragmatic breathing, which will relax you even further.

Consider taking up meditation or yoga.

One of the best ways to calm an anxious mind is by doing meditative activities, such as yoga or tai chi. Aside from the physical benefits, these activities will help you achieve clarity and calmness, which moves with you throughout the day.

Take responsibility for yourself and what you need.

This is one of the most important points in this section. If you feel anxious, think of it as a sign that something is not right. It might be something real or only something you fear. Whichever it is, take the steps to work on it or manage it as soon as possible. If you need a break, take one. If you need to call a friend, do it. If you need quiet time, plan it. Make certain you are always working from a place of get- ting what you need.

Engage in relaxing hobbies or activities.

This may sound pretty basic, but too often, my clients who are most anxious are also involved in activities and hobbies that stress them out. For example, a relaxing hobby might mean watching sports on TV. For most people, it does not include watching the local or world news. Other relaxing hobbies might be craft projects, cooking, antiquing, or reading – anything that allows you to get away from your thoughts and fears for a while.

Spend time with friends.

We are social creatures – we need to spend time with other people. We need laughter, warmth, and touch to feel our best. Strive to maintain your friendships – don't isolate yourself.

Keep to your word. Deliver what you promise.

One of the most powerful and simplest concepts to reduce anxiety is to practice keeping your word. Many times, we promise ourselves that we will do something – and then we don't do it, which makes us feel worse! We get caught up in a cycle of rationalization and feeling stuck. You can change this, but only by promising to do what you're sure you will do.

Bonus Exercise:

Go through one whole day following through on what you've promised yourself. If you said you'd take a few hours off, do it. If you said you'd complete one paragraph of writing, do it.

Just make sure your goals are doable in the given time frame. You'll feel much better and more energetic when you keep your word to yourself.

Do the best you can – all the time. And recognize this about yourself.

Realize that you're always doing the best you can. You are a motivated, bright, high achiever – otherwise you likely wouldn't be pursuing a Ph.D. in the first place. You are always doing the best you can – and you will feel immensely relieved when you realize this. As I tell my clients, "If you knew a better way, wouldn't you already be doing it?"

Find yourself doing something right and acknowledge it.

Too often, we focus on all the "bad" things, or the "not good enough" things. This makes us feel more anxious, because we feel worse and worse about ourselves. Instead, begin to shift your focus to all the things you do right each day. Whether it's eating breakfast or brushing your teeth – acknowledge your successes.

Bonus Tip:

For one day, keep track of all the things you do right. Aim to list one hundred items. Keep the list with you and refer to it whenever you feel low.

Don't spend too much time obsessing about the future or brooding about the past.

The *major* cause of anxiety is worry about the future or brooding about the past. We think "could have done this, could have done that" and "this might not happen, and that might not happen" and "that would be terrible and horrible" and "what if... what if… what if…"

This type of thinking is a natural habit, but it is *not* good for you. None of us can change the past, and we can't know what the future holds. So do your best to stay in the present, focused on the task currently in front of you. I know this can be challenging, but you will benefit immensely from the sense of calm, ease, and peacefulness that you obtain from living in the present moment.

Remember that FEAR is "False Evidence Appearing Real."

One of my mentors, Terri Levine, shared this idea with me. Many times, what we are afraid of is not really true!

One way to tell whether or not your fears are real: if you're constructing elaborate "If- then" scenarios, it's *not* a real fear. Think back to a time when you were truly afraid. That is true fear. Now think about something worrying that hasn't happened yet, or is already past. That is not true fear. A major difference is that you feel *true* fear in your body. *False* fear is generated by over-thinking, over-planning, or over-worrying. It has no physiological basis.

Don't jump to conclusions.

This is a tough one! Too often, we think we "know" the reason something has occurred or the way a situation will unfold. We usually don't. Keep your focus on the present, and allow the future to present itself to you in good time. Reacting appropriately is fine – overreacting is never helpful.

Tell your Inner Critic to "Shut Up!"

When you get really caught up in worrying and feeling bad, try telling your Inner Critic to *shut up*. Say this out loud, or write it down a hundred times. It *will* help you clear your mind if you do it honestly, with feeling.

Schedule a "worry hour" each day.

In this hour, you do nothing but worry. You worry about your life, your writing, your pets, your family, your friends, your laundry, your dishes, and the state of your relationship – anything at all. Worry, worry, worry. After the end of the hour, you're not allowed to worry any more for the rest of the day. You've already used up all your worry minutes.

Make a huge, long, exhaustive list of all the things you *don't* want. Then make an equally long list of all the

things you DO want. You will feel better after this release.

This is another anxiety releasing exercise. When you feel really anxious, write a huge, long list of all the things you *don't* want: bad hair, to work on your dissertation, to call your advisor, world hunger, poor economy – whatever. Add things to this list until you've written everything that you *don't* want to do or have happen. Then take a new sheet of paper and begin a second list of all the positive outcomes and wishes you *do* want. This simple technique can help you shift your energy into a more productive place.

SECTION XIII: THE WRITING PHASE

Recognize that this is probably a brand- new experience for you. Give yourself per- mission to learn as you go.

Rough drafts are called this for a reason. It is unlikely that you will find your writing style, rhythm, or voice in the early stages of writing. Write anyway, and allow yourself to progress and learn as you go.

You can write the sections of your dissertation in any order you choose. In fact, it's sometimes easier *not* to write it straight through from beginning to end.

You may choose to start with the most difficult chapters, to get them out of your way. Or you may choose to write the section you find most interesting, to get you started and motivated. Choose to write in whatever order feels best. There are no rules.

Have some convenient way of organizing your ideas or notes.

I suggest that my clients consider using index (note) cards. These are simple, portable, and easier to search through than an ever- expanding computer file.

If you feel stuck, try some of the creativity boosters mentioned in this book to get you moving again.

Actively using this book, not just reading it, will help you overcome any setbacks. It's all about keeping up the forward momentum. Go to Section VII: Boosting Creativity to begin overcoming the barriers to your progress. What have you got to lose?

If you just don't feel like writing, try writing about why you don't feel like writing.

Get these feelings out of your way. If you can allow yourself to fully express all your feelings, you will clear them out of your sys- tem, freeing your mind and energy up to get to work.

If you get tired of working on one kind of task, try to work in sections, and on more than one type of task at a time.

For example, you may want to take notes on one section, begin writing that section, and then start taking notes on the next section concurrent to the writing. Mixing up the kinds of tasks may help keep your interest level high.

Aim for two to four hours per day of good writing time.

Any more than this and you're probably expanding your work unnecessarily. More is not always better.

Aim to write about one to two pages an hour, at least.

This will keep you moving at an adequate pace and you will feel glad to have concrete proof of your productivity. Students who take longer than this to write a page (especially when they have already completed research) may be running into perfectionism, which needs to be addressed.

Plan to write as early in the day as possible. Get it done and off your mind.

One of my clients brings his laptop computer into bed with him and writes a few paragraphs before he even gets out of bed.

Save certain tasks for days when you don't feel like writing, but want to keep up your momentum.

Tasks like formatting, filing, spacing, fonts, and creating headers are great for those days when the ideas aren't flowing smoothly, but you want to make progress anyway.

Don't get bogged down in any one section for too long.

If you are stuck in writing something, make some notes about what you're trying to say, and go on to something else.

Carry a few pages of work to be edited when you go to doctor's appointments or other places where you might have to spend time waiting.

You can revise and improve your work while you wait.

Remind yourself that the dissertation is the gateway to the rest of your life. It's _not_ the major work of your career.

This may help alleviate some of the anxiety surrounding creation of the finished work.

To keep track of your revisions, try using color.

This idea was suggested by one of my clients: Use various colored papers or colored inks to define revisions or text versions. For example, draft number one might be printed on blue paper or in blue ink, draft number two on yellow paper or in red ink, etc. This way, you can keep track of which pages belong to which revision. Another idea is to "name" each draft differently and place this "name" in the headers and footers for that page. For example, draft one might be called "first attempt draft" and this designation would appear on all first draft pages. Second draft might be called "Oh No, not again" which would be the designation defining all the pages in this draft.

Keep track of your writing goals in terms of your overall timeline to completion.

Don't get discouraged if you don't meet a monthly total – just try to catch up by the next time.

Try to write something every day.

Integrating the writing into your daily life will help the process flow more smoothly.

SECTION XIV: MANAGING FEEDBACK

Realize that "negative" feedback is not about you or your abilities.

Feedback is just a series of words. Only our perception or belief about these words causes us to perceive them as positive or negative. Words are not personal.

Practice getting feedback often – it won't be so shocking and upsetting.

Often, graduate students complete large sections of work before turning these in for feedback or comments. This, unfortunately, can lead to a vicious cycle of delaying feed- back, feeling bad when you get it, and then delaying feedback further as a result. If you can find a way to send your work in regularly throughout the process, receiving feedback won't be so anxiety-provoking or shocking.

Think of each comment as one more step to a completed dissertation.

It is sometimes helpful to consider that each comment brings you one step closer to a completed dissertation. So, rather than dreading the comments look at them as hints or tips pointing you down the road to success.

Ask for comments in the way that is most comfortable for you.

This may be via a meeting to go over the material, an email that you can read at your leisure, or a phone call, so that you can benefit from hearing your advisor's inflection and tone. Choosing the way that works best for you will make feedback easier to manage.

Know that anxiety about receiving feed- back is very common.

All of us feel anxious and worried when we are being evaluated. Remind yourself that even your professors get nervous when being reviewed.

Ask for clarification if you don't under- stand or can't figure something out.

After receiving feedback, be sure to ask for further clarification if you don't understand the comments. It is better to be as clear as possible before you start revising.

If you're really nervous about getting feedback, have someone else read the comments first. This can give you time to pre- pare yourself.

Ask a trusted friend, your spouse, significant other, or coach to skim the comments before you read them. This can give you time to prepare yourself and gives you some preliminary feedback to allay your fears.

Realize that you have some degree of choice in what changes you make to your work.

Be sure to clarify which comments are advised, and which are suggested. This is your project, and you have the right to retain parts that you feel are important. Work with your advisor to help him or her see your perspective.

Realize that each advisor will have different standards for an acceptable dissertation.

If you want to know your advisor's preferred approach, ask him or her. Also read through and study other dissertations he or she has chaired.

Focus as much on the positive feedback as the negative feedback.

Too often, we skip right over the positive feedback we receive. Yes, it is important to look at areas for improvement, but it's equally important to acknowledge what you are doing well. This will be helpful in the future, when you need to discuss your strengths.

Take a day or two "off" after receiving feedback.

Give yourself time to absorb the comments, manage them, and return to work more productively.

Realize that learning to accept feedback constructively is an important skill – both professionally and personally.

The sooner you learn to accept feedback constructively, the better it will be for you.

Remind yourself that this is probably not the first or the last time that you will be told something difficult to hear.

Consider this as "practice" and "muscle building" for other life events.

Don't be afraid to ask for support when you receive feedback.

It helps to bounce your thoughts and ideas off others – a friend, spouse, colleague, or coach.

Try to think of the feedback in the long term.

Will it really matter in one or five or ten years? If not,

allow yourself to let it go.

SECTION XV: DEALING WITH DISAPPOINTMENT

Accept that you will be disappointed, at least once, during the dissertation process.

It is very difficult, if not impossible, to work closely with others on a project of this importance and scope for a year (or more) and not be disappointed. If you accept that this is likely to happen, that knowledge may help you to manage the disappointment more easily.

Express your feelings.

When you have been disappointed or hurt by someone, it is best to express your feelings to him or her as soon as possible. If that feels too difficult or overwhelming, express your feelings to someone else. Get those negative feelings (hurt, anger, betrayal, or sadness) out of your way.

Look to your past for clues for how you have successfully managed previous disappointments.

Use these strategies to help you manage your disappointment now. Coping strategies may include physical activity, journaling, cleaning your house, calling friends, or taking the day off. Whatever has worked in the past is a good place to start.

Allow yourself to forgive.

The main point of the dissertation process is to finish the project and move on to the rest of your life. Holding anger, grudges, or bitterness will interfere with this. Do your best to forgive, let go, and move on. There are better things waiting for you on the other side of the Ph.D.

Write an angry letter – but don't send it.

One technique that can be helpful is writing an angry letter to the person who has disappointed you. Get all your anger, hurt, and betrayal out on paper, then burn or shred the letter. Many people find this very cathartic.

Ask for support if you feel overwhelmed.

Many times, disappointment can trigger past feelings of sadness, anger, and betrayal. If you feel overwhelmed by what has occurred, ask for support as soon as possible.

Know what you need, and ask for it.

Sometimes, we expect others to read our minds, or to know our expectations, instead of simply sharing our needs with them. If you need your advisor to call you back – say so. If you need an answer by a certain day or time, request it. Take responsibility for getting your needs met as often as possible.

As soon as you can, try to view the disappointment from a different perspective.

Although it is not always obvious, a disappointment may contain some sort of hidden gift or meaning that will be helpful to identify. Find the underlying meaning or lesson, and you will dispel the negative feelings.

Be aware of your expectations of others, and be able to release these if necessary.

Most often, we are disappointed by others when we have certain expectations of them that they do not meet. To deal with your disappointment, examine and change your expectations.

For example, one of my clients was struggling with working with her advisor. She felt let down and betrayed by the advisor's lack of consistency and follow-through. We spent several sessions discussing all possible actions or avenues. What we ultimately came up with was that the advisor was over- whelmed, overbooked, and overloaded, and that my client couldn't change this. However, she, my client, could change her expectations. Once she stopped having certain expectations of her advisor, my client found it easier to manage her disappointment. My client didn't necessarily *like* the way things happened, but she no longer felt so upset and helpless each time similar events occurred.

Practice being flexible whenever possible.

A flexible attitude is a great skill to practice and develop, both for the dissertation and for life. Being flexible will allow you to change, to accept that things will change, and to find the optimal path for your own personal success. Incidentally, if you're able to be flexible, you will also decrease potentially damaging perfectionism.

Keep track of your disappointment(s) so you know what *not* to do when you work with or advise others.

Probably the main complaint I have heard is of advisors not being as responsive or avail- able as my clients would like. I ask my clients to keep track of behaviors that upset and annoy them, so that they can be certain not to repeat these behaviors when they move into academic faculty positions and begin to advise others. Even if you can't change what is happening in the present, there is some peace of mind in being able to shape the future.

Set reasonable deadlines for yourself and others. Communicate these to others as soon as possible.

Quite often, my clients do not discuss their plans or goals with their advisors or committees, and then feel disappointed and hurt when events proceed in unplanned directions. A great way to avoid this is to communicate, clearly, what your plans are.

For example, try saying to your advisor, "I want to finish my dissertation within one year. Is this something we can work towards?" If you ask questions like this early on, you and the people you're working with can ensure you're all on the "same page." When everyone is in agreement, the work will proceed more quickly and smoothly.

Practice extra self-care during this time.

When we are hurt or upset, we need to take extra special

care of ourselves. Unfortunately, many of us "drop the ball" when we're feeling poorly. The sooner you take good care of yourself, the sooner you'll feel better.

Start over, in this moment.

When you commit to a fresh start, you can move forward without being burdened by anger, guilt, or resentment from the past. You can't change the past, so why not move on from it as quickly as possible?

Be persistent! Keep trying!

Whatever you do, please don't give up. You can and will finish your degree and move forward on your life journey.

SECTION XVI: THE DISSERTATION DEFENSE

Attend between two and four defenses in your department to see how it's done.

Reading all about defenses won't prepare you adequately for the way they are conducted in your particular department. Attend several, so you have some idea of what to expect. It's also a good way to support your friends and colleagues. If this is not possible, contact newly defended colleagues for input and information, then stage your own practice defenses.

Conduct practice defenses – discuss your research with colleagues, family, and friends.

Like any presentation, the words will flow more smoothly and easily the more you practice. Also, practice will help you ensure your presentation is coherent, understandable, and fits within the timeframe and other guidelines recommended by your department.

Utilize all presentations (at conferences, job talks, etc.) as opportunities to refine your defense presentation.

Again, the goal of completing your dissertation becomes

easier when all your activities are supporting it. Use conference presentations, job talks, and colloquia as opportunities to improve your materials and your presentation skills.

Prepare a twenty- to thirty-minute presentation of your dissertation and tape record it.

You will be able to refine your speaking, notice excessive "ahhs" and "uhmms," and sound more polished in the final presentation.

Practice your presentation in front of a mirror.

This will help you improve your presentation and look more polished, as you notice and fix excessive hand gestures or nervous behaviors.

If you're not sure how to answer a question, take a breath and pause for a few seconds.

Eventually you will have to answer the question, most likely, but you can give your- self a few seconds to consider it fully and pre- pare a complete answer. Don't feel rushed or harried to jump in before your thoughts are fully organized.

Remember to use deep breathing and be aware of your

toes on the floor.

This helps you remain both "centered" and "grounded".

Remind yourself that you're not defending alone.

Ideally, your advisor and members of the committee will be supportive of you and will be there to help you finish. If this is not the case, remind yourself of your family, friends, and any Higher Power whom you feel might be supporting you at this stressful time.

Be as relaxed as you can about accepting input during the defense. Don't promise to make the requested changes, but thank people for their input during the process.

Remind yourself that feedback, questions, and comments are not intended as attacks on your competence or capacity. Accept new input gracefully, without making promises to add or remove anything from your final product.

Some phrase such as, "Thank you, that's very interesting. I will consider it further," will allow you to respond graciously to comments without committing yourself to any specific revisions.

Create a system of note cards or other reminders to help you stay focused during your presentation.

Some people have used large index cards, transparencies, or wall charts. Try a few systems in advance to see what works best for you. Practice with your chosen system several times before the defense date.

Tape record your defense.

This was suggested by one of my former clients. She found that it allowed her to retain all information from the defense needed to make suggested changes, without having to write furiously or miss something during the process.

On the day of the defense, call in reinforcements.

Have your best friends, most supportive colleagues, your spouse/significant other, parents, relatives, anyone and everyone you might want to utilize for support.

Plan for feelings of hostility, anger, or defensiveness to creep up during the defense process.

Knowing that these feelings are likely to occur – and are normal reactions to stress – may help you manage them appropriately.

Celebrate on a grand scale when it's all over – congratulate yourself on a job well done!

The best way to keep having success is to keep celebrating success!

SECTION XVII: WHAT NOW?

Transitioning to Post Dissertation Life

Make any corrections, notes, and changes as soon as possible after the defense.

Get the dissertation fully completed, down to the last signature, the last submission, start the final binding – be completely done with it!

Expect to feel strange or let down.

You have devoted a great deal of time and energy to this process. It is completely understandable to feel strange or let down once it leaves your life.

Practice getting used to being addressed as "Doctor."

This is the fun part!

Write down your experiences as a way to help others through this process.

You likely will be advising someone else in the future, and it will be helpful to have these reflections.

Consider giving yourself (or accepting) a huge reward or treat for finishing.

Have some fun! Celebrate this ending in style!

If possible, give yourself some open time and space between finishing and moving on.

You will need some time to adjust and re-equilibrate. Two weeks at least!

Spread the word!

Let everyone know that you've finished. Acknowledge and thank them for their support.

Start dreaming about the future.

What now? The road to your life is calling!

If possible, plan to attend the formal graduation ceremony.

Being "hooded" on stage and introduced as "Doctor" at graduation is one of my favorite memories! It also provided a symbol of closure for this part of my life. And it was a wonderful day to spend surrounded by family and friends.

If you found this book helpful, consider passing it on to a junior colleague, with additional hints, tips, or advice.

Have a lot of fun.

You probably "put off" time spent with your family, friends, or doing your favorite activities. Start making up for lost time!

Consider sharing your success with other students through online forums or newsletters.

It is both motivational and inspiring to read about people just like you overcoming the challenges of completing their degrees.

List all the personality traits you needed to complete your degree (flexibility, tenacity, wisdom, dedication, just to name a few….) and write these down somewhere.

Refer to this list if you ever doubt that you have what it takes to succeed.

Take some time to reflect.

Spend some time reflecting on how you've changed and grown through this process, what you've learned about yourself, and about others. This will help you integrate this life experience more fully.

Congratulate yourself.

You're amazing!

ABOUT THE AUTHOR

Dr. Rachna D. Jain

Licensed Psychologist & Dissertation Coach

Rachna obtained her doctoral degree in 1998 from the University of Denver's Graduate School of Professional Psychology. Her dissertation focused on the personality correlates of marital satisfaction. She interned at the Pittsburgh VA Consortium, and is licensed as a psychologist in the State of Maryland.

Rachna is also the Editor of the *All But Dissertation Survival Guide*, a twice-monthly email newsletter focused on helping graduate students complete their doctoral dissertations.

As a coach, Rachna has worked with many graduate students to help them complete their degrees quickly and easily.

APPENDIX

How to create a timeline to dissertation completion

1) Start at the bottom #, by listing when the dissertation is due in your department.

2) Work backwards, using the timeframes in the sample below to create your target dates

3) Once you have created your target dates, work forward, by setting goals to span the distance from where you are now, to where you will be at your first target date.

Start proposal and Human Subjects Application (if Human Subjects applicable)

Aug 15 (2 months)

Send proposal into committee for review

Oct 15 (1 month)

Send application for Human Subjects Review (if applicable)

Nov 15 (after proposal accepted)

Start collecting data, or writing chapters

Dec 15 (start here, allot 3 months)

Start Data Analysis, Review of Results,

Mar 15 (1 month)

Start writing Discussion, completed by

Apr 15 (1 month)

Start writing Conclusions and Final Chapter

May 15 (1 month)

Turn paper into Committee for review

Jun 15 (1 month)

Corrections and revisions based on feedback

July 15 (2 weeks)

Prepare for Defense

Aug 1 (2 weeks)

Defense

Aug 15

This is intended as a sample only; actual dates and

deadlines will vary based on your department.

www.ingramcontent.com/pod-product-compliance
Lightning Source LLC
Chambersburg PA
CBHW071446030726
47593CB00003B/912